Drawing Animals Shape by Shape

Drawing Animals Shape by Shape

Create Cartoon Animals with Circles, Squares, Rectangles, & Triangles

sixth&spring
books

NEW YORK

DRAWING WITH Christopher Hart

An imprint of
Sixth&Spring Books
104 West 27th Street
New York, NY 10001

Managing Editor
LAURA COOKE

Editor
LAURA COOKE

Art Director
DIANE LAMPHRON

Book Design
EMILY JONES

Cover Design
JOE VIOR
ALICIA MACKIN

Editorial Assistant
SARAH THIENEMAN

Vice President
TRISHA MALCOLM

Publisher
CAROLINE KILMER

Creative Director
JOE VIOR

Production Manager
DAVID JOINNIDES

President
ART JOINNIDES

Chairman
JAY STEIN

Library of Congress Cataloging-in-Publication Data
Hart, Christopher, 1957-
  Drawing animals shape by shape : create cartoon animals with circles, squares, rectangles and triangles / Christopher Hart. -- First Edition.
    pages cm. -- (Drawing Shape by Shape/Draw Anything Series ; #5)
    ISBN 978-1-936096-95-4 (spiral bound)
    1. Animals in art--Juvenile literature.
    2. Cartooning--Technique--Juvenile literature. I. Title.
    NC1764.8.A54H3795 2015
    741.5'1--dc23

13
• • •

Please visit Christopher Hart at
christopherhartbooks.com and on
YouTube at **www.youtube.com/chrishartbooks**.

FOR MY DAUGHTERS, ISABELLA AND FRANCESCA

4

What's Inside

Let's Have Some Fun!

Welcome, artists!

In this new book on drawing animals from simple shapes, I'll show

you how to create your favorite animals in no time using easy-to-follow steps.

You'll find so many great species to choose from—everything from fluffy

woodland creatures to elephants, pets, lions, dinosaurs, sea creatures, and

more. If there's an animal you want to draw, chances are you'll find it in

this book. Each animal drawing begins with a simple shape such as a square,

circle, rectangle, oval, or triangle. (You can draw sketchy

shapes—they don't need to be perfect.)

Step-by-step, I'll show you how to add a line here, and then a line there, until you end up with a complete drawing.

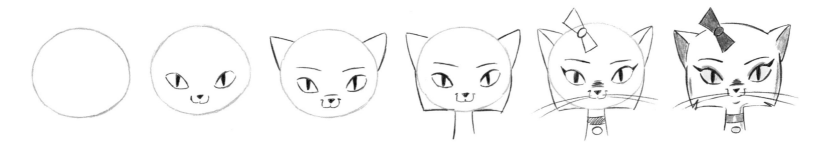

You'll also learn how to combine basic shapes. Learning to draw has never been so much fun. All you need is a pencil, and you're ready to go. Let's get started now!

Happy Drawing!
Christopher Hart

Shape Templates

If you need a little help drawing circles, semi-circles, ovals,

triangles, rectangles, or squares, use these shapes as guides for

practice. You'll be drawing your own zoo of animals in no time!

Dogs

ARf! ARf! Are you a  lover?

If so, you'll find lots of popular pooches to draw in this

chapter, including a sweet , a noble , and

a posh . It's easy to draw a of any kind using

a few simple shapes. Let's get started!

Smiling Pooch

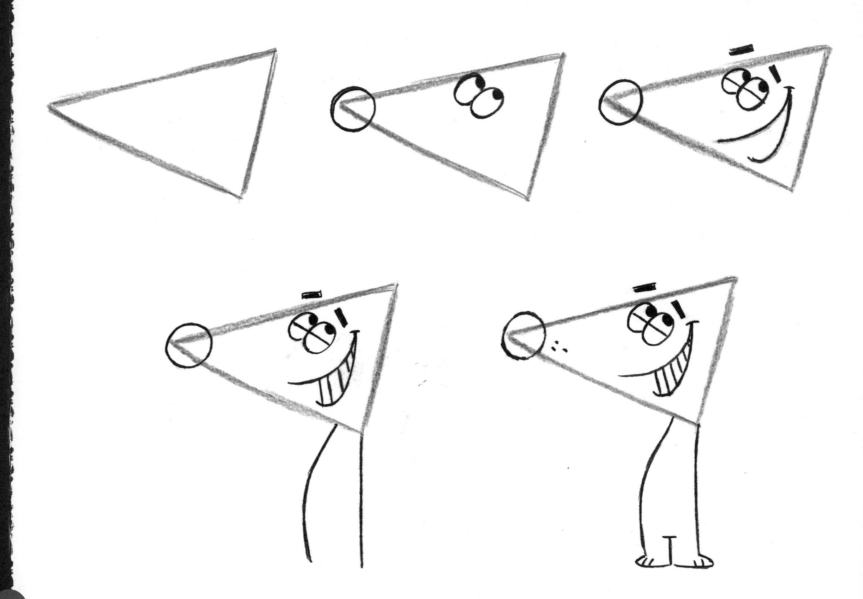

Sparky

DOZER

Fluffy

DuDLey

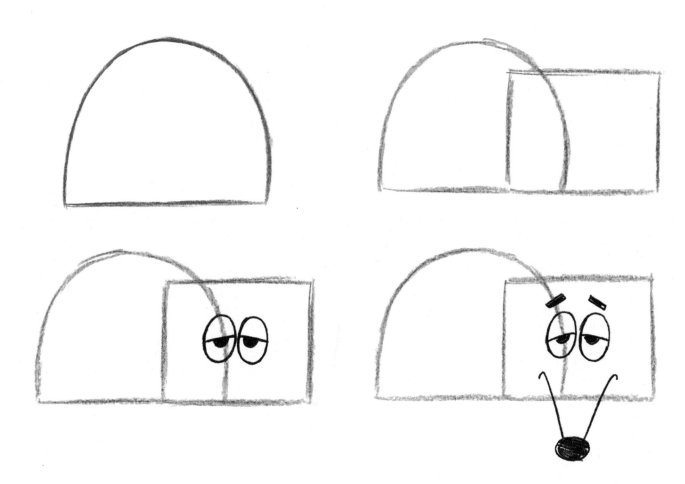

Fido

Combine shapes!

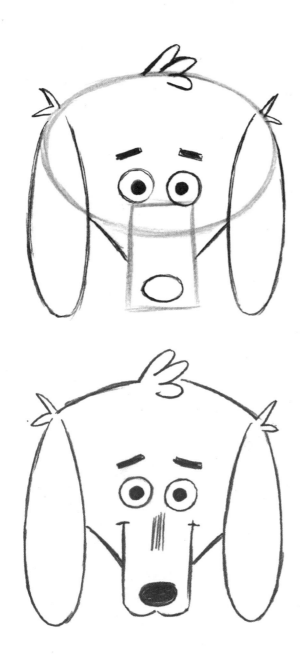

Rover

Princess

Scottie

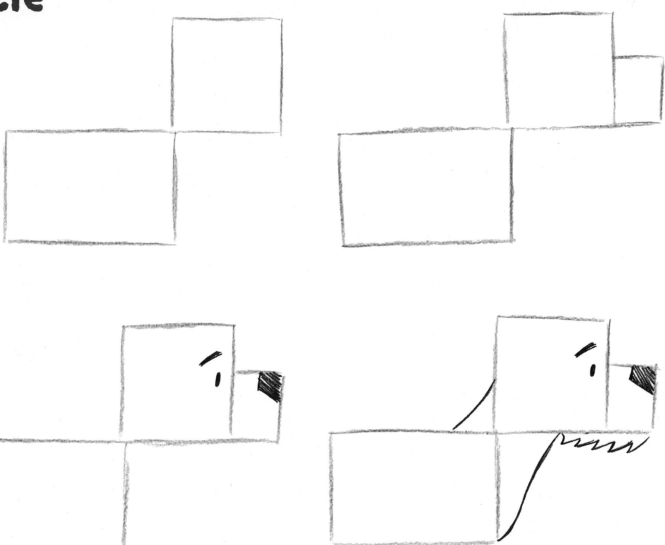

Pinky

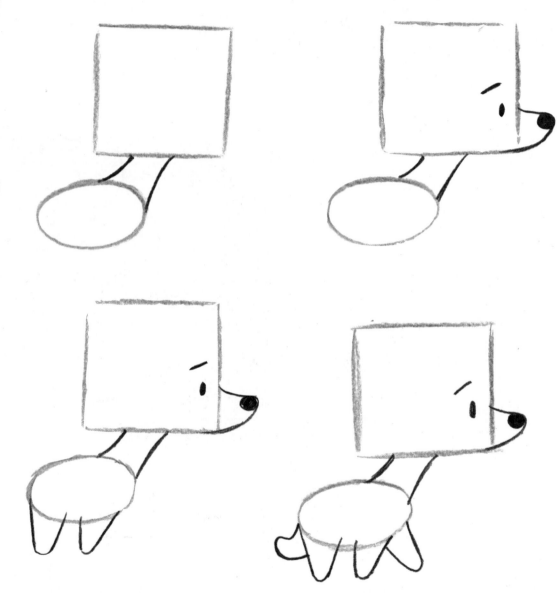

Cats

Meow! Maybe you're a  person instead.

These fluffy pets have lots of personality, ranging

from a regal  to a surprised . You'll learn

to draw these plus a playful , a stubborn ,

and many more feline friends.

MR. Waffles

HuGS

WHISKERS

Sneakers

Duchess

Gizmo

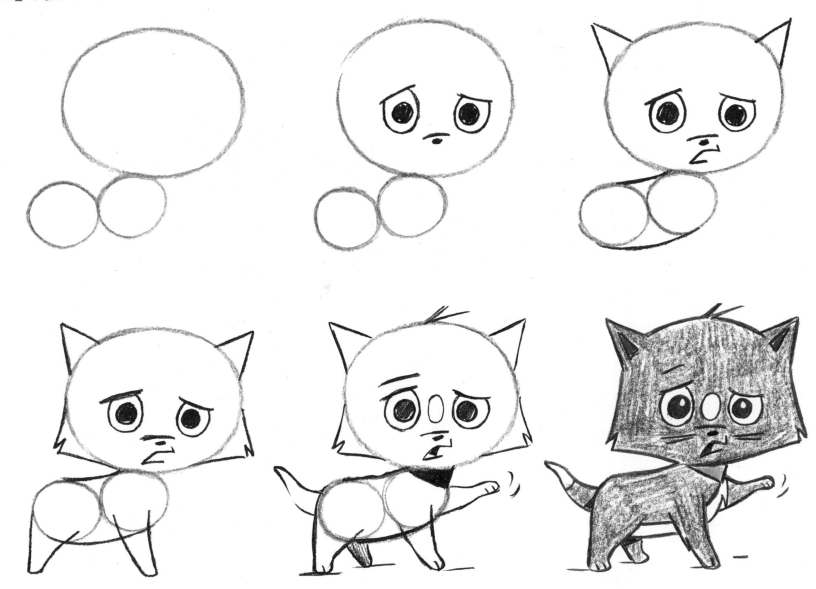

Snowball

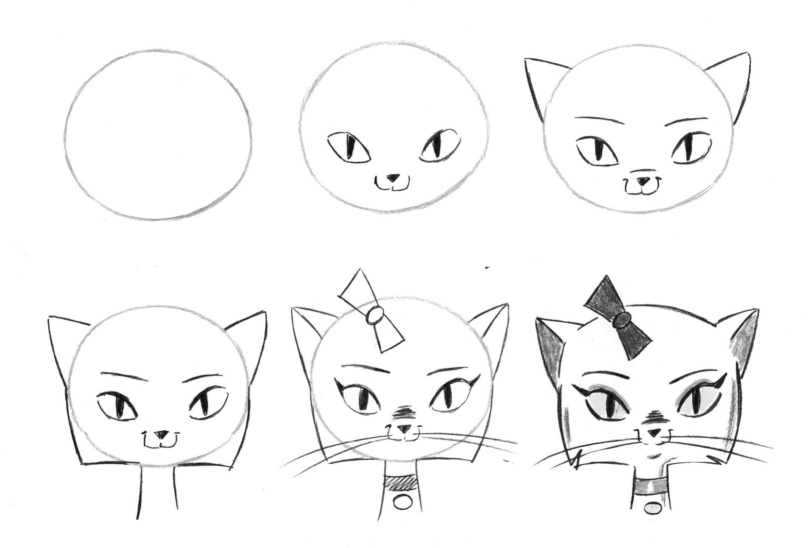

OScaR

Rascal

Ginger

On the Farm

Oink! Moo! Baa!

Whether it's a portly , a happy ,

or a wooly , farm animals are familiar favorites.

They offer a lot of variety too, from a tiny to a

brawny . But despite their differences, we start

to draw each one the same way: with a basic shape.

Pig

Cow

Galloping Horse

RooSteR

Brawny Bull

Baby Chick

Sheep

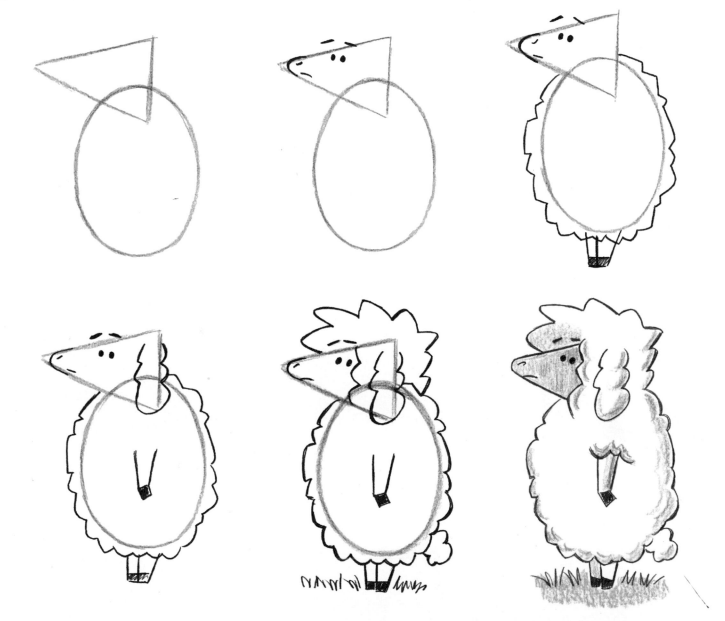

Duck

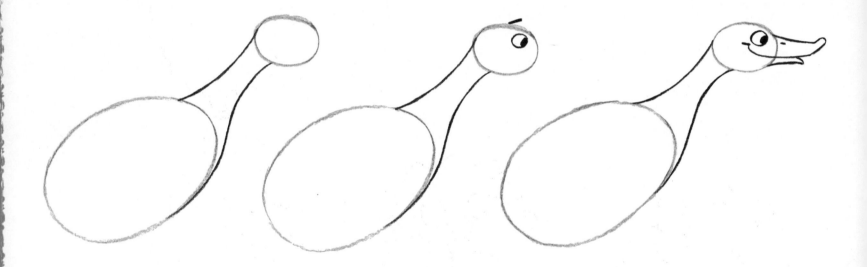

Stallion

Goat

WOODLAND CREATURES

Awww! Woodland creatures are sooo cute!

Think of a plump  or a friendly 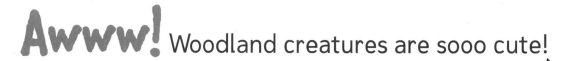 .

This serene setting is teeming with interesting critters to draw, including a brown , a dainty , and even a bad-tempered 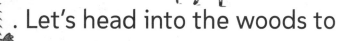 . Let's head into the woods to begin drawing these cute and quiet creatures now.

Fox

Raccoon

Brown Bear

PORCUPINE

Boar

Moose

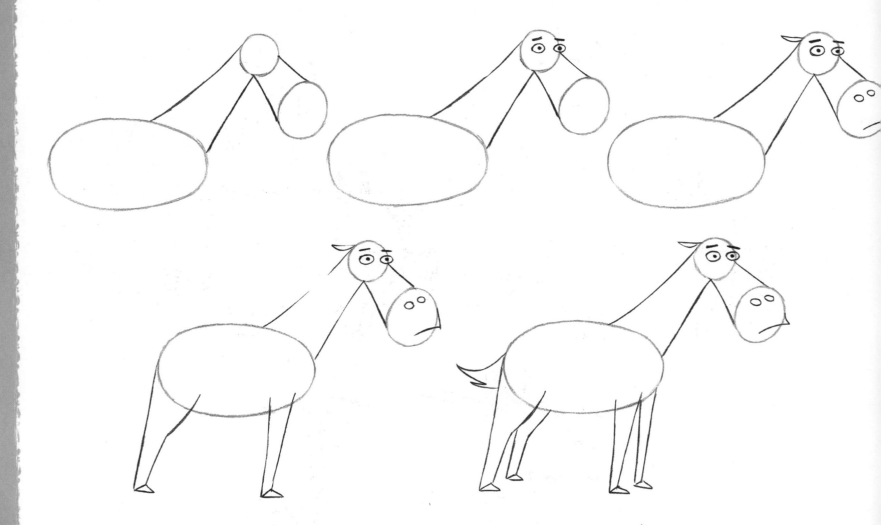

Funny Bunny

DeeR

Boxy Bear

Pointy

On Safari

Roar! The word "safari" always makes a proud

leap to mind. Or perhaps you think of a striped .

Learn to draw these along with a shifty , a happy

, an enormous , and other amazing

African animals in this fun chapter.

Monkey

Lion

Zebra

Timid Tiger

Leopard

Giraffe

ELePHant

PROUD LION

Black Panther

Hippopotamus

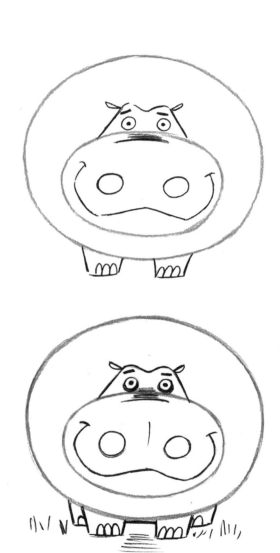

RhinoceROS

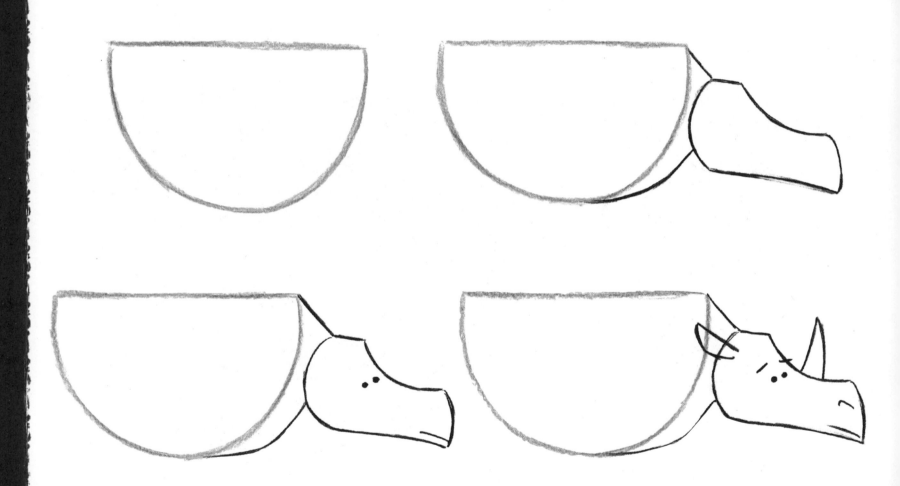

Feathered Friends

Hoot! Chirp! Squawk!

There are so many different types of 🐦s.

Draw a wise 🦉 or a gloomy 🦜. Sketch

a frosty 🐧 or a colorful 🦩. Find your favorite

feathered friends here and let your drawings take flight!

Owl

Turkey

CHEEP CHEEP

Gloomy Parrot

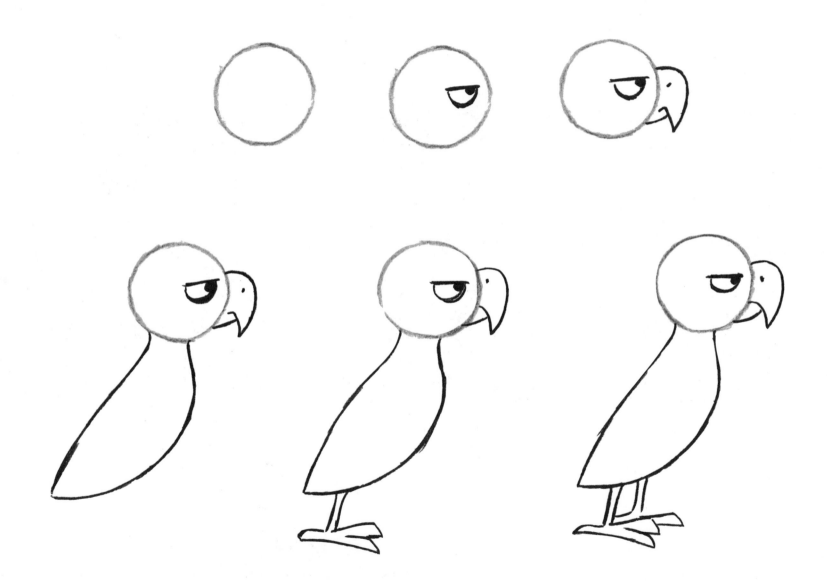

Perky Penguin

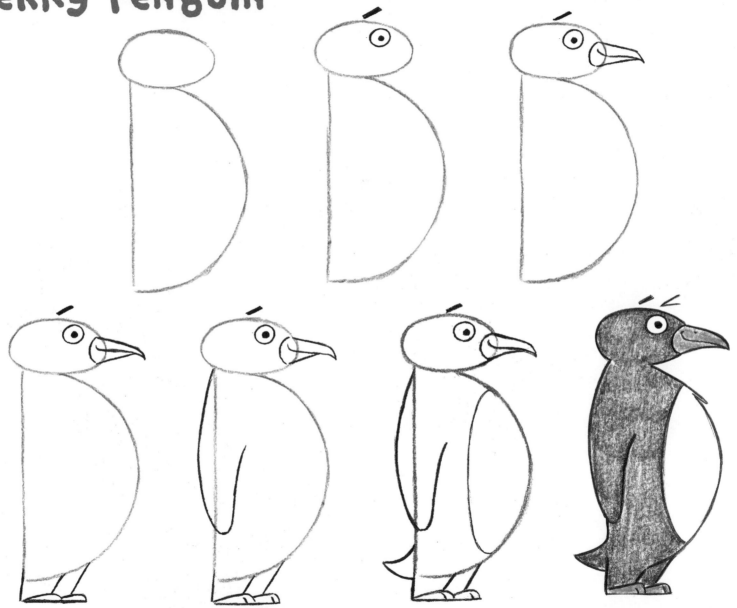

Brave Eagle

Hummingbird

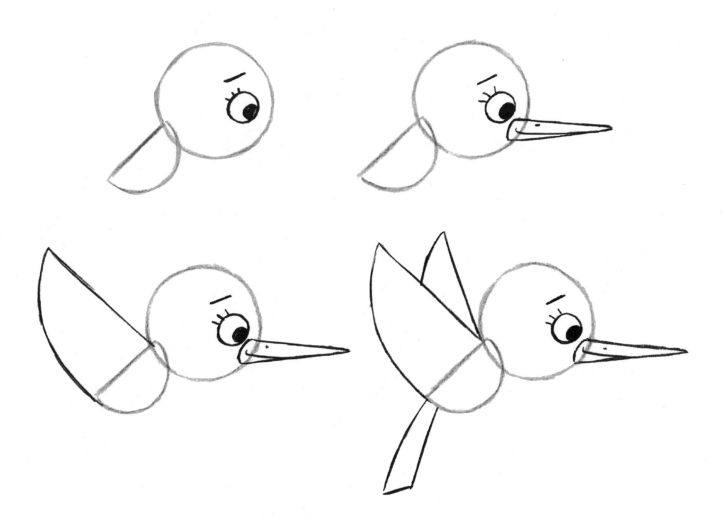

Duckling

Happy Bluebird

Toucan

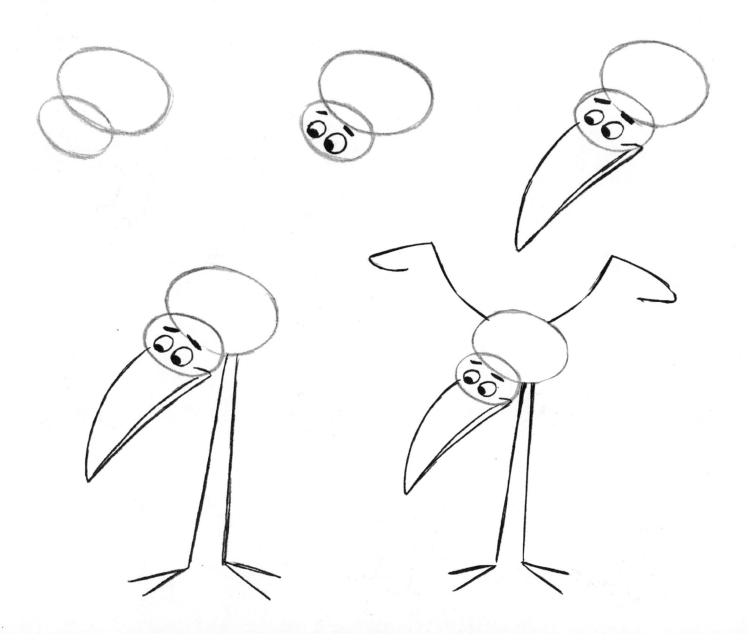

SCARED OSTRICH

Baby Penguin

In the Water

SPLASH! Let's dive into this diverse collection

of sea creatures. Learn to draw a tropical  swimming

by the shore, an adorable  in its icy home, or a

whopping  rising to the surface. You'll also find

a chummy , a cunning , and more!

Sneaky Shark

TROPICAL FISH

Funny Fish

Baby Seal

DOLPHIN

Fishy

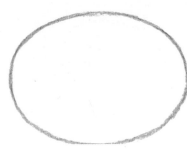

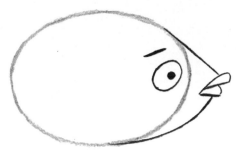

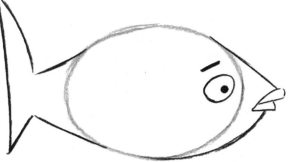

Lobster

WHALE

Stealthy Swimmer

ReptiLes anD Bugs

SLitHeR! Buzz!

From the swampy  to the busy , reptiles

and bugs are fascinating creatures. And fun to draw, too!

Whether it's a leisurely , a beautiful 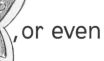, or even

a hungry , when you start with a simple shape,

you can draw almost anything!

Iguana Running!

Anxious Ant

Tortoise

ALLiGatoR

KOMODO DRAGON

Bee Happy

DRAGONFLY

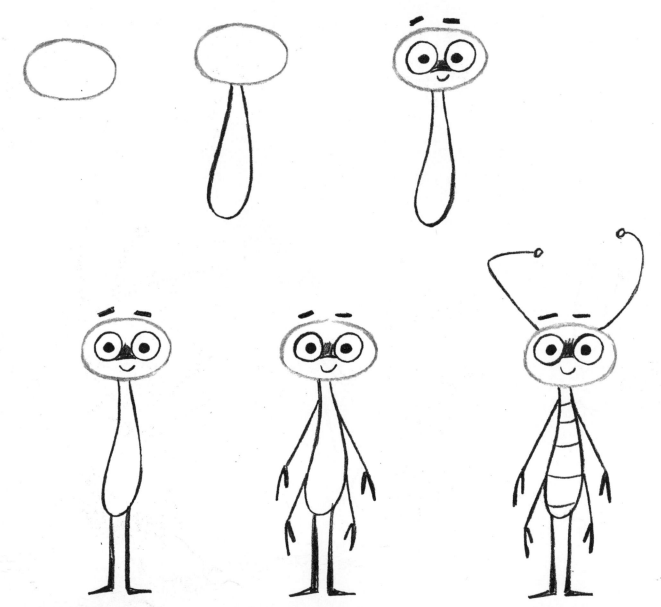

Busy Bug

Speedy Turtle

(Huff-Puff!)

Butterfly

DINOSAURS

CHOMP, CHOMP! STOMP, STOMP!

Now we're ready to draw some real giants. Have some

fun with a fascinating 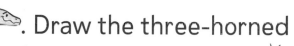. Draw the three-horned

, the plant-eating 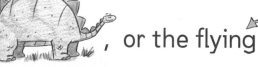, or the flying .

And don't forget the fearsome , everyone's favorite!

Apatosaurus

Triceratops

ANKYLOSAURUS

T. Rex

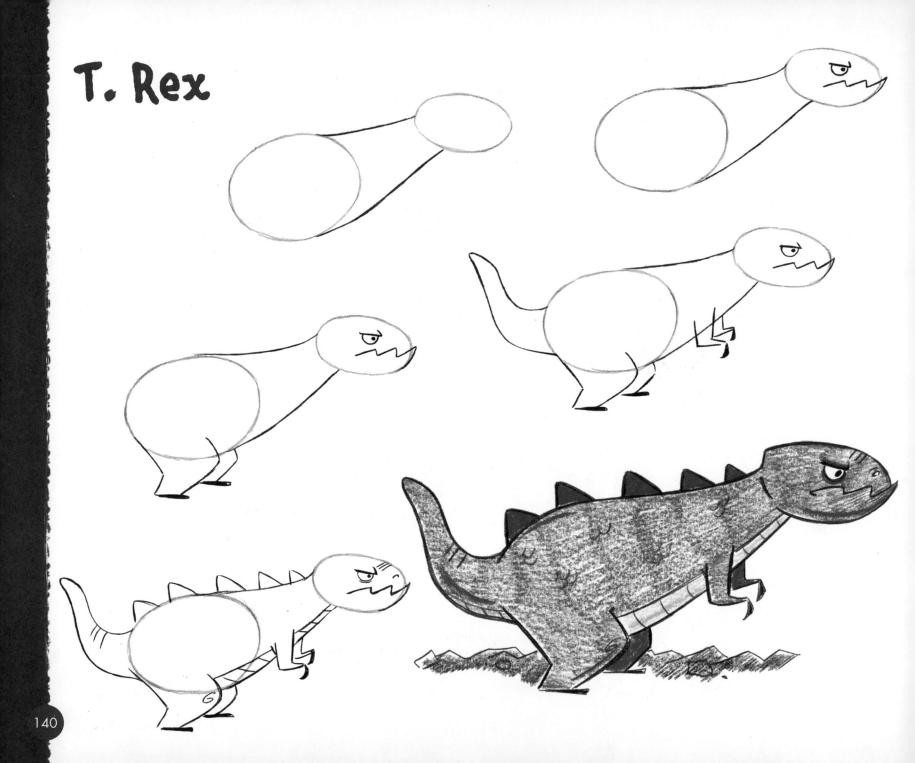

Spinosaurus

HuNGRy GiaNt

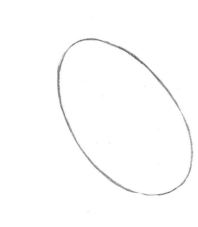

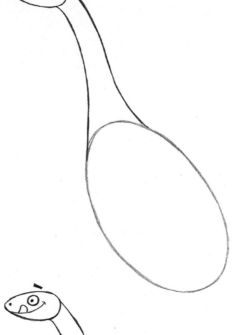

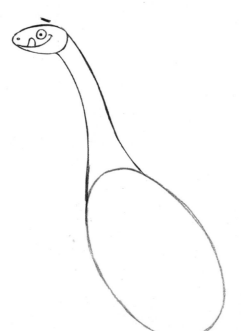

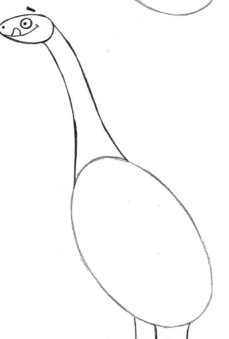

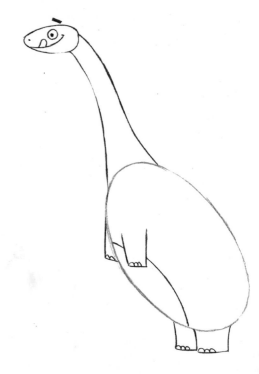

DimetRODON

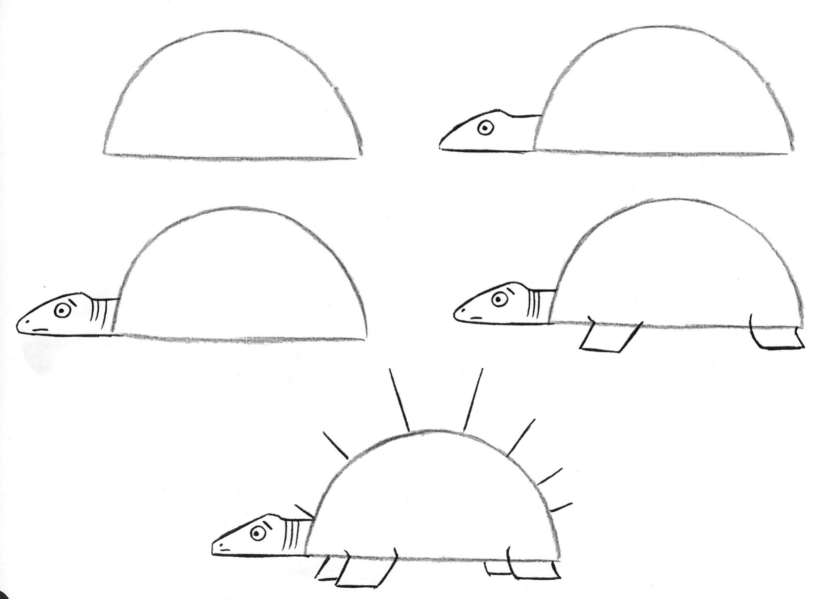

PteRodActyl

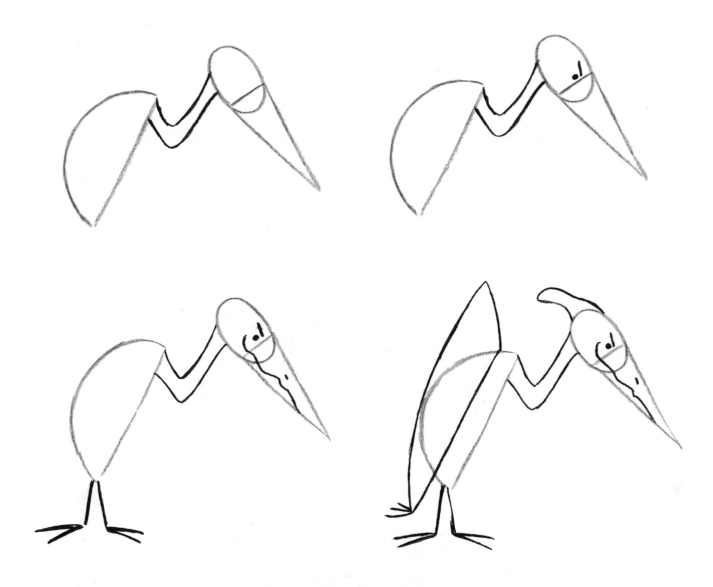

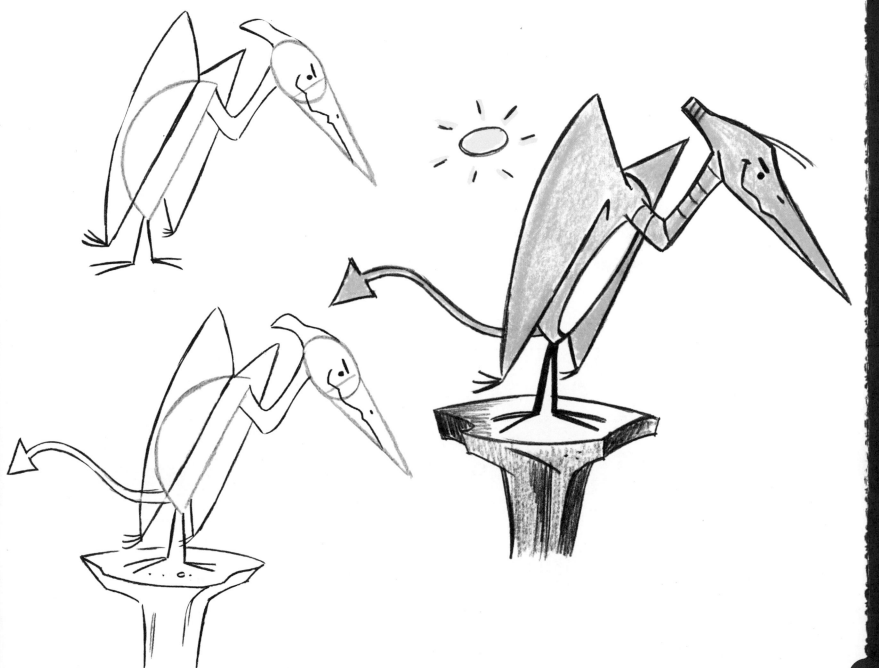

MoRe
FuN
AnimaLs

Woof! Ribbit! Squeak!

This is where you can let your imagination go.

Here you'll find a magical and a dancing .

There's a cool keeping warm with a scarf and a

powerful keeping fit with some dumbbells. You'll even

find a creative to match your own inner artist.

When you start drawing with a simple shape,

the possibilities are endless!

Bodybuilding Dog

151

Friendly Frog

Pretty CHIPMUNK

Out for a Stroll

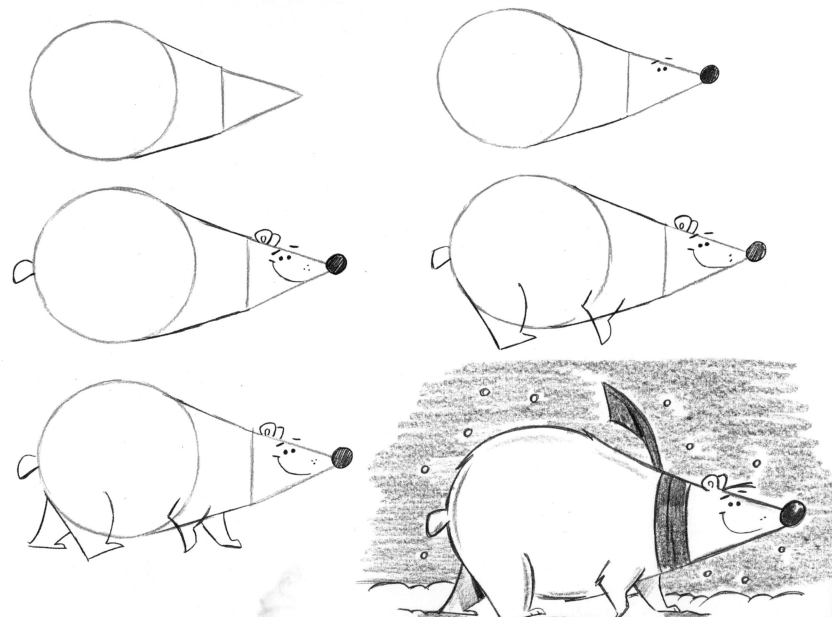

Nearsighted Squirrel

Art-Loving Hippo

Hunny-Bunny

Hello there, Bear!

BLUSHING BUFFALO

Mischievous Mouse

Playful Pachyderm

Beaver Ballerina

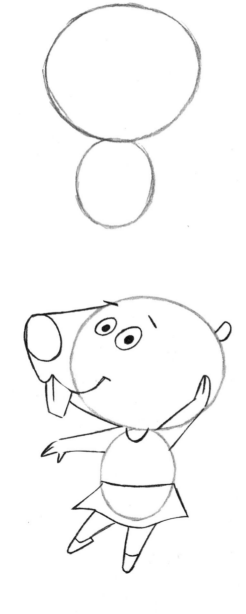

DOWNHILL DoGGie

WHOOSH!

Magical Unicorn

Varsity Moose

Bear Buddy

Looking for your favorite animal?
Check the alphabetical list to see which page it's on.

Index

DRAW even MORe fun Characters
USinG SimPLe CiRCLes, tRianGLeS, anD SQuaReS!

DRAW A CIRCLe

DRAW

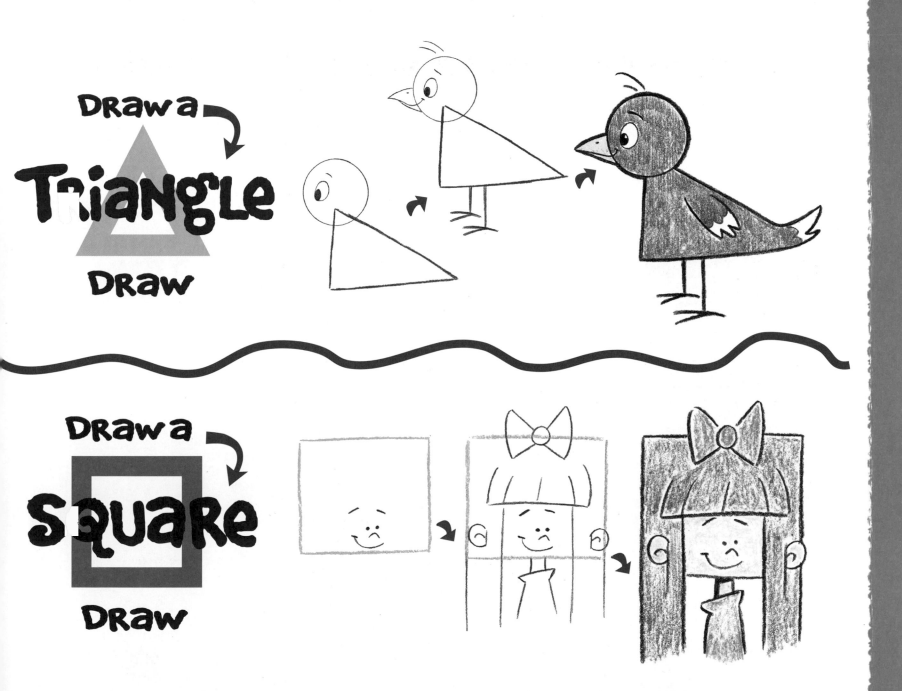

Draw a **Triangle** Draw

Draw a **Square** Draw

AvailabLe wherever books are sold or at sixthandspringbooks.com.

Now that you can draw with simple shapes, what's next?